Professional Development

B. Vincent

Published by RWG Publishing, 2021.

While every precaution has been taken in the preparation of this book, the publisher assumes no responsibility for errors or omissions, or for damages resulting from the use of the information contained herein.

PROFESSIONAL DEVELOPMENT

First edition. June 10, 2021.

Written by B. Vincent.

Also by B. Vincent

Affiliate Marketing
Affiliate Marketing

Standalone
Affiliate Recruiting
Business Layoffs & Firings
Business and Entrepreneur Guide
Business Remote Workforce
Career Transition
Project Management
Precision Targeting
Professional Development

Professional Development

Someone once said, income seldom exceeds personal development. And John Maxwell tells us, growth is the great separator between those who succeed and those who don't. And it's true, no one reaches the top unless they've developed themselves personally and professionally. If you want to climb the corporate ladder or take your organization to new heights, you must always be bettering yourself. But how do we stay on top of professional development in our busy lives, how do we incorporate growth into our daily routines. In this course, we're going to show you how to do exactly that.

76% of employees are constantly looking for opportunities for career growth.

74% of employees feel that they are not reaching their full potential. 44% of employees admit that a lack of career growth and advancement opportunities is their main source of stress. These statistics show that professional development is an increasingly important area that businesses should focus on.

Our course is going to consist of a series of critical discussion points. These are designed to cover this broad topic as thoroughly as possible, to encourage growth in these vital areas, and to facilitate a real and fruitful discussion, within your organization, about how you can each improve on this essential characteristic, both at work and in your personal lives in general.

Some of these will be pretty lengthy and some will be relatively straightforward and brief. At the very end of this roadmap, comes the most important final step. Discussion time do not skip this. This is the most important part of this training.

When you finish this course, you need to spend at least an hour or so, going over the questions we supply at the end, as a group, whoever's the head honcho in the group should designate a facilitator, whose responsibility it is, that each question is covered and that everyone, time permitting, is able to have their say. Make sure all contributions are valued, all suggestions considered, and all opinions are respected. So, let's move into the first discussion point.

Utilize available resources, as an employee, your main objective is to mature more as a professional. This means that you constantly find ways to improve, searching for every medium that offers development. Fortunately, there are a lot of resources available that you can take full advantage of.

In fact, these resources can be available within your company, without you even costing a penny. This may include in-house training and development programs. On the other hand, you can ask your company if they offer reimbursements for paid courses outside of your workplace. Every year, there are a handful of conferences and events that take place. Make it your goal to attend each one. However, there are other low-cost options that offer more flexibility, so you can study at your own pace. This can include online programs, recorded webinars, and books. Taking full advantage of these resources gives you a diverse range of knowledge that strengthens your fundamentals and expands your skillset.

Join professional organizations, whatever work you may have, there's a good chance that a professional organization exists in your field, professional organizations or associations that act as an umbrella for employees, who are working in the same or similar fields. These groups strive to foster the profession by hosting meetings and events, as well as conducting research for continuous learning.

They also endeavor to maintain standards by assisting their members, providing resources for professional development in promoting their field to the government and community. Do you want to be a part of such an affiliation? Take a look at the professional associations within your field. For example, if you're a certified public accountant or a similar position in finance, you can join the American Institute of CPAs AICPA Institute of Management Accountants IMA, or the American Payroll Association, APA, to name a few. Note that some organizations may require annual membership fees, while others are absolutely free to join. In either case, joining such organizations gives you access to exclusive resources and tools that you won't find elsewhere. These can include webcasts, mentorship programs, and regular updates of the latest trends in your profession. Moreover, being a part of an association expands your network, providing you more opportunities for career advancement.

Receive stretch assignments, stretch assignments are tasks given to employees that are beyond their current roles and skills. These tasks are designed to test their limits, allowing them to stretch developmentally. By placing them in uncomfortable situations you force them to think outside the box, thus helping them to learn and grow. Here are some examples of stretch assignments, participate in the company's strategic planning process, join a team dealing with conflict, delivering a presentation to a VIP client, implement a new company scheme reviving a failed product or launching a new product, oversee people from different cultures, gender, racial or ethnic backgrounds, leading the implementation of new tools to replace manual processes, performing data analysis to find business efficiencies, write a policy statement, stretch assignments, expose you to real-world situations.

The way you carry out these assignments help managers determine if you have what it takes to become a potential leader in your organization. Doing stretch assignments can also count as a form of support to your overseers, as they usually have too much on their plate. When you accept these tasks, you can give them a chance to offload so they can focus more on the most important tasks on their part.

Shadow, a colleague, job shadowing, is an activity in which his staff from one area of the organization has the opportunity to work alongside other staff in a different area of the organization and gain insight from the experience. When you shadow other colleagues, you'll get to learn from the experiences of other colleagues, appreciate other needs and priorities, outside of your work role, understand how other departments work, discern how other roles support the organization with job shadowing, you'll get to learn new skills, qualities and related competencies that can help you to develop. Moreover, being exposed to different areas within the organization can help them gain a deeper appreciation of how other departments work, and how their roles contribute to the success of the organization. This in turn will boost your morale, and to help you grow more as a professional,

Receive feedback, receiving feedback is the most straightforward way to grow professionally. When you receive clear-cut feedback, you can easily pinpoint what areas you need to improve on. However, in order to receive feedback effectively, you first need to develop the proper mindset. It's important to understand that the purpose of receiving feedback is to have access to a broad range of perspectives.

Instead of trusting your somehow biased outlook of yourself, having a different POV is the most effective way to identify your true strengths and development areas. Although you may find it to be uncomfortable, you know well that getting feedback can be both humbling and rewarding.

So now the question is, how can you receive feedback effectively? Here are some tips: active listening, fully concentrate and understand the person giving feedback by not interrupting, be aware of your body language. Avoid looking distracted and bored for it sends a negative message. Be open, be receptive to new ideas and suggestions, reflect, assess the value of feedback, and determine what to do with it, follow up, after implementing the suggestions, set up another meeting to discuss the changes made.

Receive feedback, receiving feedback is the most straightforward way to grow professionally. When you receive clear-cut feedback, you can easily pinpoint what areas you need to improve on. However, in order to receive feedback effectively, you first need to develop the proper mindset. It's important to understand that the purpose of receiving feedback is to have access to a broad range of perspectives.

Instead of trusting your somehow biased outlook of yourself, having a different POV is the most effective way to identify your true strengths and development areas. Although you may find it to be uncomfortable, you know well that getting feedback can be both humbling and rewarding.

So now the question is, how can you receive feedback effectively? Here are some tips. Active listening, fully concentrate and understand the person giving feedback by not interrupting, be aware of your body language. Avoid looking distracted and bored for it sends a negative message. Be open, be receptive to new ideas and suggestions, reflect, assess the value of feedback, and determine what to do with it, follow up after implementing the suggestions, set up another meeting to discuss the changes made.

Find a mentor, we all need a helping hand in order to develop, this is where a mentor comes in. A mentor is an accomplished person that gives you help or advice to the less experienced and oftentimes younger professionals. A mentor usually shares his own success story and motivates individuals to reach or even surpass that level of success. They provide guidance, emotional support, as well as assisting individuals in setting goals, exploring careers, and identifying resources.

The most obvious reason to get a mentor is to learn from the experience. Mentors have been there and done that. That's why you can learn a lot from their failures and accomplishments. Moreover, they share practical real-world advice, which you won't learn in any textbooks. Having a mentor also gives you reassurance. When you have someone that guides you and you can share your worries with, it reassures you that you will succeed. Having someone by your side boosts your self-confidence, helping you to view every challenge as an opportunity to improve.

Where can you find a mentor? Here are some places where you can start your search, your current network, inside your company, professional organizations, events, entrepreneur hotspots, and LinkedIn. Finding the right mentor not only helps you mature professionally, but they can also be a great medium for expanding your network. In fact, they would likely even share their own network with you, giving you more opportunities that you wouldn't otherwise have.

Build a professional network, networking isn't just an exchange of business cards with different people. It's about setting up long-term mutually beneficial relationships with the people you connect with. Building your network creates a lot of opportunities to receive further support, knowledge, and advice on how to grow professionally and personally.

How can you build a professional network? Here are some practical tips: find the right people, you don't need to join every professional organization or attend every event to build your network. After all, your goal is not to connect to every person you meet. Instead, you need to focus on finding the right people that you know will help you make a difference in your career.

Create Win-Win situations, networking isn't a one-sided relationship. It's vital that you and the other party will mutually benefit with your connection. If you benefit more than the other person, they will feel used, establish clear expectations right from the start. Make the first move, instead of waiting for people to ask you for help. Why not be the one to offer some support. This will make your connections grateful and would certainly want to return the favor. Serve as a connector, you're not the only one who can benefit from networking. You can also use these opportunities to introduce others to other people who can then benefit from one another. This creates stronger rapport and will leave you fulfilling.

Practice time management, time management is paramount to grow as a professional. When you manage your time wisely, you will finish every milestone on schedule, and reach every goal promptly. Besides prioritizing, you can manage your time by conditioning yourself mentally. Peter Bregman, a best-selling author popularized a book entitled 18 minutes, which talks about finding your focus, so you can get the right things done. By using 18 minutes of your time each day, you can combat distractions in-game productivity.

Here's how 18 minutes all sums up, morning, five minutes. Start the day by thinking about what can be done to achieve your goal today, then take those things off your to-do list and schedule them into your calendar. A minute per work hour, eight minutes, as you go about your eight to five job, you need to refocus yourself. Set an alarm every hour, every time the alarm goes off, reflect on what have you done in the past hour. Ask yourself, have I spent the last hour doing something productive. Evening, five minutes, after you've turned off your computer, take a moment to meditate. Take a deep breath and recap how your day went.

Another way to make sure you're using your time wisely is by eliminating distractions in the workplace. Our phones can be a real menace from getting work done, you won't even notice that you've spent three hours of your day just checking your phone. What you can do is to set your phone to a setting that you know won't be bothered. Some people even turn off their phones when needed. Another good tip would be to hide these distractions from you. You can do this by putting it in a place beyond your reach. This can be the bottom part of your drawer or inside the deepest pockets of your bag. Also make sure that your work area is conducive to productivity, close any tabs regarding social media, online shopping, or any other platforms that can tempt you to bide your time.

Develop a sense of urgency, a mature professional values time and makes the most out of every second. This is why having a sense of urgency is vital for development. Having a sense of urgency means that you're fully present at the moment. In other words, you're mindful of your current situation and are ready to act promptly and decisively, though not worrying too much about what may happen in the future. Having a sense of urgency will prevent you from overthinking. Instead, you focus on the present, taking one day at a time. A worker with a sense of urgency understands how fast paced the business world is, so he or she strives to keep ahead of everyone else. To develop a sense of urgency, you need a proactive approach, a proactive person is like a chess player in order to win. You need to think a few steps ahead. The same is true when dealing with tasks. To manage time, you need to think ahead to see what needs to get done. Discipline, urgency starts in the mind. Discipline requires tremendous self-control. When you're locked into your goals, you won't get distracted. Optimism and determination, optimism provides confidence when things get tough, while determination provides the courage to keep moving forward.

Right down your goals, Dr. Gail Matthews from the Dominican University of California surveyed 267 people and found out that you are 42% more likely to achieve your goals if you write them down. Why is that so, it affects you psychologically, physically writing down your goals provides tangibility, giving you a clear picture of what you want to accomplish. The process of writing down goals on paper enhances your mental capabilities by forcing you to strategize, review your progress, and regularly brainstorm new ideas on how to achieve them. Seeing your goals written down on a regular basis, serves as a daily reminder for you to keep moving forward.

Create an action plan development without planning is a big no-no. If you want to grow effectively, you need to create a solid action plan to reach your goals. Sadly, this step has often been overlooked. Some people are so focused on the outcome that they forget to plan all the steps needed to achieve that goal.

In fact, some even set goals without even knowing how to achieve them. To create an action plan, it should contain these fundamentals, a clearly outlined description of the goal, a summary of tasks that needs to be accomplished, people delegated on carrying out each task, milestones, deadlines, resources needed to complete each task, measures to evaluate progress. Having an action plan provides a clear direction of how you want to achieve each goal. It helps you to stay committed throughout each day. Furthermore, having an action plan helps you prioritize tasks effectively.

Set priorities, a lot of professionals remained developmentally stagnant due to having poor prioritization. Setting priorities ineffectively can affect your effectiveness and deficiency in the workplace. This can drag you down from growing. In order to get things done in time, you need to set your priorities. An important thing to remember is that tasks have different needs. So, you need to prioritize accordingly. Avoid skipping tasks, jumping from one task to another will not only waste your time, but it will also prevent you from getting any work done. You can prioritize tasks effectively by using the ABCDE method, popularized by Brian Tracy, the ABCDE method allows you to gauge the level of importance for each task, so you can prioritize them according to their urgency. Here's how the ABCDE method works. A, very important, these are the MITs are the most important tasks that you currently have. These tasks should be your highest priority for it would be the basis of your success. B, important, these are tasks that are valuable as well, just to a lesser degree, such tasks will lead to minor negative consequences when neglected. C, nice to do, these items are the ones that have no consequences at all, whether you do them or not. D, delegate, these are tasks that you can assign to someone, usually by outsourcing. E, eliminate, these are illusionary to dos, that are in reality actually junk. You should get rid of these ASAP.

Develop keystone habits, professionals who succeed in the business world, are often recognized for having keystone habits. Keystone habits, as defined by Charles Duhigg are small changes or habits that people introduce into their routines that unintentionally carry over into other aspects of their lives. As an employee, acquiring these metaphoric habits, transform you to be the best version of yourself, so you can perform better while maintaining proper work-life balance. Looking to develop keystone habits, here are some examples: daily exercise, sleeping early, writing a daily journal, cooking, donating to charity, spending quality time with loved ones, meditation, practicing gratitude. These keystone habits serve as building blocks for professional development, these routines strengthen your physical, mental, and emotional state, improving your overall welfare.

Conduct a personal SWOT analysis, a SWOT analysis is a notable strategic technique that helps an individual assess his skills and capabilities. The primary objective of SWOT is to help individuals develop a full awareness of the internal and external factors that can affect their careers. A SWOT analysis must be done before goal setting, to ensure that the goals you set complement your specific needs, here's the breakdown of SWOT. Strengths, what am I good at? weaknesses, what areas do I need to improve? Opportunities, what possibilities are in store for me? Threats, what can potentially harm me from growing professionally? A SWOT analysis is beneficial, as it serves your framework for career advancement. It recognizes core strengths, reverses the weaknesses, maximizes opportunities, and avoids threats. By reviewing your performances, you can identify what areas you should focus on.

And now it's discussion time, the most important part of this training, whoever's the head honcho in the group should designate a facilitator, whose responsibility it is that each question you see on your screen is covered and that everyone, time permitting, is able to have their say. Make sure all contributions are valued, all suggestions considered, and all opinions are respected.

Don't miss out!

Visit the website below and you can sign up to receive emails whenever B. Vincent publishes a new book. There's no charge and no obligation.

https://books2read.com/r/B-A-QWUO-BKLPB

BOOKS 2 READ

Connecting independent readers to independent writers.

.

Also by B. Vincent

Affiliate Marketing
Affiliate Marketing

Standalone
Affiliate Recruiting
Business Layoffs & Firings
Business and Entrepreneur Guide
Business Remote Workforce
Career Transition
Project Management
Precision Targeting
Professional Development

About the Publisher

Accepting manuscripts in the most categories. We love to help people get their words available to the world.

Revival Waves of Glory focus is to provide more options to be published. We do traditional paperbacks, hardcovers, audio books and ebooks all over the world. A traditional royalty-based publisher that offers self-publishing options, Revival Waves provides a very author friendly and transparent publishing process, with President Bill Vincent involved in the full process of your book. Send us your manuscript and we will contact you as soon as possible.

Contact: Bill Vincent at rwgpublishing@yahoo.com www.rwgpublishing.com